SOUL RISE

Best wishes
Adam ♡

SOUL RISE

SOUL EXPRESSIONS

ADAM BERRY

Matador
Unit E2 Airfield Business Park,
Harrison Road, Market Harborough,
Leicestershire. LE16 7WB
Tel: 0116 2792299
Email: books@troubador.co.uk
Web: www.troubador.co.uk/matador
Twitter: @matadorbooks

ISBN 978 1803131 191

British Library Cataloguing in Publication Data.
A catalogue record for this book is available from the British Library.

Printed and bound in the UK by TJ Books Ltd, Padstow, Cornwall
Typeset in 10.5pt Minion Pro by Troubador Publishing Ltd, Leicester, UK

Matador is an imprint of Troubador Publishing Ltd

MIX
Paper from
responsible sources
FSC
www.fsc.org
FSC® C013056

Dedicated to my paternal father Peter Lord, 'like a father'
Neil Ferguson, my beautiful big sister Sarah Berry and my
dear friends and wise souls Alan Wilson & Big Mike.

All now in the spirit world but who made the biggest impact on my life
with their love, support and kindness and who still inspire me today.

THANK YOU

There are just too many to thank for taking the leap to
publish my work, but I wanted to mention:

All of my friends and family who have supported me,
listened to my poems, shared them and encouraged me.

Thank you to my wonderful parents Barbara and Tony (Barbie Doll
and TB) as without their love and support I would not be here.

Thank you to Shaun, my soulmate, lover and best friend for
being my biggest cheerleader and sharing this life with me.

Thank you to Mavis Pittilla and Jean Else for helping
me to find my voice and my inspiration.

Clare Castle – My bestie, who has been with me through thick and thin; 'everyone needs a Clare in their life'.

Suzette Carlyle – Thorley – for your love & support throughout and being a catalyst in encouraging me to share my work.

Martin, Darren, Marlene, June, Jackie, Jean, Kim, Edith, Helen, Joanne, Trevor, Annie, Cath, Christine, Laurie, Janet, Jeff, Tyrone, Nicole, Rukhsana, Belinda, Gill, Daniel and countless others who have been a great support throughout this project.

CONTENTS

INTRODUCTION

Soul Rise is a compilation of work inspired by life and events in a way that could be relatable to all. We each have our individual philosophies of soul and stories to be told. This book started with a poem and evolved into expressions of the soul, to touch souls. After each expression, you are given the opportunity to personally share your own reflections with how the words may have touched, moved or affected you in some way. This book invites you into a deeper understanding of self and of others.

It is designed so you can share the expressions at your favourite spiritual gatherings and communities or maybe with your friends, family or anyone you feel may benefit from the words or a particular page for the changing times in life that we all face.

FOREWORD

I am delighted that Adam has been able to reflect upon many significant and special times in his life and cathartically release his innermost expressions through his poetry.

He has also provided a unique opportunity for you to join him, on your own journey, and to let your own 'Soul Rise' by absorbing his work and reflecting upon your journey through life.

As you react to his words and situations and begin to release your own expressions, your eternal partner, your soul, will find peace and joy.

Mavis Pittilla

ROUNDABOUT

My life is like a roundabout, spinning so so fast,
Turning round so violently, how long will all this last?
Too fast for you to jump on, and too fast for me to leave,
People on board with bad intention, whilst my heart is on my sleeve.

Sometimes the brake is needed, to cause this ride to jam,
To fling off all those people, that just don't give a damn.
As it starts to turn again, this carousel is much lighter,
This ride of life it seems, has become so much brighter.
It's not so violent… and has slowed down…
It was my choice, how fast it spun round.

The people that were flung off, it now transpires to see,
Their finger was on the spinning button, pushing and controlling me,
This roundabout called life, that was seemingly such a chore,
Is now a life respectfully, that I truly do adore.

REFLECTIONS

THE BOTTLE MY FRIEND

How can this happen, how can this be?
The life that I was living, felt like my destiny.
The struggles, the traumas, the pain & the strain,
My heart full of tortures, all dull & just rain.

My delusional friend, that I drink & I drink,
Not wanting sessions to end, sweats, shakes & on the brink.
The delusions were real, and I believed what I said,
When all this was no deal, that I would never be dead,
From this way of life, I was unfortunate to know,
Clenching hold of the bottle, seasons, sun through to snow.

But this destiny was death, the bottle I had trusted,
It was killing me sharply; this friend had been busted.
I was awakened to realities, beyond my comprehension,
The spiritual truths, that relieved all the tension.
This bottle put down, my so-called friend was gone,
A new life was born, helping me move on.

I thank the voice that called to me,
That came from deep within,
My soul had suffered enough now,
It was time to live & win.

REFLECTIONS

RISE

The sun will always set,
and darkness will loom,
But not complete darkness,
due to the light of the moon.
As the morning draws closer,
and you open up your eyes,
The darkness has gone,
because the sun will always rise.

REFLECTIONS

MIRROR

When I look into the mirror, what do I see?
The man that was a boy, looking back at me,
Not through beard or height,
But with the eyes, that shining light,
The brightness depends on the time that he spends,
On the times that have passed, with a half or full glass,
Glass of fear & shame, glass of cheer & game,
This life is not the same,
Boy to man becoming sane,
Sane I say it loosely though,
As this man still has a way to go,
Learning, growing and moving on,
Embracing the soul and being at one.

REFLECTIONS

HAPPY

As you left this land, on your onward flight,
Leaving our world, in black and no light,
Your presence was love, and always so true,
Things will never be the same; we will always miss you.

Your little reminders, of memories so dear,
Through music or TV, the signs are so clear.
The blackness can lighten, when we feel you close,
Not close as we once knew, but with a new host.

A host of angels, that you are now part of,
With your beautiful voice, singing your heart out.
As you lift off high, and you leave this land,
Remembering our times, now in the universal hands.

As the time ticks further, in this crazy thing called life,
You are always nearer, when in our times of strife,
So blessed are we, to know this truth,
That this darkness we feel, would really upset you.

So we wish you well, with all things bright,
And colours so precious, not black or white,
You were never dull! You wouldn't want us to be down!
So it's time to be happy for you, and turn this frown around.

REFLECTIONS

SOUL RISE

And through the ages and test of time,
The only sacrifices uncovered, were mine,
Disabled in thoughts, and restricted in mind,
Believing in what you wanted to believe,
Feeling left behind,
Under a dark spell? Venturing through misty woods,
Hit by the branches, and never feeling good.
Then, a spark from within ignited a shock,
The soul starts to rise, changing my luck.
The foundation, my salvation, my God or my love,
The spark from within, a sure sign from above.
Life is for living, and it can take the school of hard knocks,
For the soul of our being, to truly rise from beneath the rock.

REFLECTIONS

PREDATOR

A story still needs to be told,
A time of a truth to no longer withhold.
You can think it will never happen to you,
To your family, or your friends.
But when a predator makes their move,
It sickens your feelings, like it never ends.
You see this person is very clever
In manipulating you in their endeavours;
They build up a false sense of security;
They groom you, and your vulnerability.
The shame and the guilt you cannot comprehend,
Of the hurt caused from the supposed friend.
They destroy the lives of the silent few,
And disillusion many with how they view you.
The preacher, the healer, the spiritual teacher;
Why couldn't we see the red flags of danger?
But slowly but surely, the flags gathered all at once,
The realisation was a rage-filled response.
I detached from you as my feelings were slander;
Prison was needed for you, life as an insider.
Multiple accounts of sexual assault… including kids,
You are a monster of the world, a sickness insipid.
The predator has an energy like no one you have ever met.
The feelings and the question mark,
The predator… you will never forget.

REFLECTIONS

NATURE

In the fields of beauty,
Where the buttercups reign,
Bright colours of yellow,
And the dew from the rain,
And where the wild roses grow,
Red, white and pinks,
A river does flow,
And the birds do sing.
The sun shines brightly,
Projecting a radiant glow
On the water flowing rapidly,
A healing place to go.
The power of light & nature,
Is a truly sacred space,
Its life and all creation,
Is a truth we must keep safe.

REFLECTIONS

NEXT CHAPTER

As you slipped away,
Into the sleepy light,
Your eternal of days,
Shines power and might.

The power of presence,
The power of soul,
Divine in your own essence,
In light of pure gold.

No pain and no sickness,
This will disappear,
Your soul will feel acceptance,
As a healing place appears.

Your light shines on,
Eternal and progressing,
Your soul in true form,
Your life you are addressing,
The life you had, the life you are,
The life to come, your journey so far.

Evolution awaiting you,
Entering a world unseen,
A page of your story ends now,
Your next chapter taking scene.

REFLECTIONS

POSITION OF TRUST

You thought you were clever,
You thought you had fooled us all,
The deviance within you,
Streamed like a waterfall,
The victims that you prowled upon,
Pretty and vulnerable women,
All quite broken and sensitive,
A shark circling whilst they were swimming,
You were there for teaching,
You had a duty of trust,
You should not have been leaching,
Your morals forever lost.
You may think you have got away with things
As time has gone on.
But a lot of people know the truth
As you act like nothing is wrong.
A predator you were, and a predator you still are.
I pray for the women that you left scarred.
However, they are lucky that you are no longer a threat.
As your next victims are already in debt.
You use and abuse for your narcissistic power,
When your victim is of no use, you are back to the prowl.
So strength to any woman that is in your life.
And spare them the dignity of being the victim wife.

REFLECTIONS

NEW WAVE

It's not out of reach, and not out of sight,
Although we all feel, like giving up on the fight.
The Great Spirit does call to us from up above,
Trying to inspire minds to act as they should,
We just have to accept that this will take time,
Trusting in the Architect's plan a day at a time.
One day we shall rejoice in a oneness for all,
A soulful renaissance of the spiritual call.
No ego to run from, and no selfish intent,
Only community and values on our time spent.
Our family, our friends, our neighbours, our lovers,
Our children, our pets, our sisters and brothers,
True kindness for all, in our thoughts and our deeds,
It's what the world craves for, and what it truly needs.
As we work on ourselves, and feel the Divine praise,
These are basic principles for a spiritualist new wave.

REFLECTIONS

THE LITTLE FIR TREE

In the midst of the woodland, of a sacred-fuelled place,
There sits a little fir tree, standing firmly in grace.
All in isolation this tree does dwell,
Embracing the silence and thriving so well.
The trees that surround and tower above,
Their leaves and their branches, sway as they should,
This could seem intimidating for other smaller trees,
But not this fir tree, it sits full of glee.
As everything changes, when the seasons come around,
The autumnal leaves fall to the ground.
A skeleton of branches are left at the scene,
Bare and stick-like, and no sign of green.
The little fir tree stands proud all year long,
Against all the elements, like the wind on a song.
Looks can be deceiving in the greater scheme of things,
We can judge our observations, with what our lives may bring,
We can react to our sensations, in a pleasant or painful way,
And feelings of isolation, can really cause dismay.
The lesson we can learn, and the true philosophy,
Is the nature of this little fir tree and its pure equanimity.

REFLECTIONS

VIPASSANA

Sitting in my meditations, observing my life's review,
Scanning all the experiences, with a new point of view,
Penetrating deeper, whilst scanning up and down,
Feeling all sensations, from my feet to my crown,
A new understanding, of what this life could be,
The nature of my existence, the real, the truth in me,
The bubbles, the tingles, the heavy gloss sensations,
The memories, the stories, and my imaginations,
Merging into presence, between awareness of the breaths,
Experiencing and observing, unconscious conscious depths.
Vipassana is a mindfulness key, giving insight to self-expression,
Dissolving years of miseries, that are responsible for depression.
It's true that nature is the truth, of all our stories to be told,
And through the guiding light within, a beautiful life can unfold.

REFLECTIONS

ACCEPTANCE

Going through life, in its twists and its turns,
Its ups and its downs, with lessons to learn,
Learning from darkness & shades through to grey,
The more we encounter, the more that we pray,
Acceptance is needed, for shades to flow bright,
Engaging forgiveness, in truth and in light.
A power unknown, a source of Divine,
A compass of life, a guidance of time,
When you forgive the unforgiven, starting with oneself,
It relieves the heavy burden, you created for yourself,
Taking responsibility for your past and your present,
Unlocks your potential future, without anger or resent.
So through all the hardships, and life's painful kicks,
Always remember, it's not always dark at six.

REFLECTIONS

RAINBOW

When rainbows form, in their beautiful ways,
The dark clouds fade, as rain hits light rays,
The sun is the mirror, of nature's wet drops,
The kaleidoscope of colour, a beauty non-stop.
Colours so vibrant, so vivid and bright,
A pot of gold maybe? But never in sight,
Rainbows have meaning to all who can see,
A sign, a hope, a message, or a meant to be,
Don't dismiss its magic, as a general occurrence,
Believe in its message, and its reassurance,
The pots of gold may never have been found,
But a rainbow's presence, is a beauty profound.

REFLECTIONS

SHARE

To share in life's darkness,
Is to share the torch of light,
When some are feeling hopeless,
And lost their future sight,
To share your deepest sorrow,
Is to share a relatable pain,
When the hardest thing is tomorrow,
Life can feel hard to maintain,
To share in all your beauty,
From within is sharing out,
To share your spirit brightly,
Helps the soul without a doubt,
When you share with the world,
One's true authentic self,
It's the light that radiates
For you, through me, from self.

REFLECTIONS

CHANGES

Our life is full of changes, even when it feels stalled.
Time and distance create movement, all within nature's law.
Feeling stuck and nothing changed, is a perception of the mind,
A prayer of help, a moment of hope, whilst in our darkest of times.
Nature teaches us, that nothing stays the same,
The seasons and the cycles, all a natural change,
Although at times we feel that we need something else to blame.
Changes that we can't control, leaving us stressed and strained.
It isn't always easy, to adapt to new life paths,
As it isn't always easy, to feel stuck in the past,
Think of caterpillars, as they turn into butterflies;
Whilst in the darkened chrysalis, do they think they're going to die?
In the dark, and feeling stuck,
Is it the end of time? Without any luck?
But within nature's calling, and a miraculous way,
The wings they start to open, breaking all the darkness away,
The beauty of the butterfly, is a caterpillar's progression,
A demonstration to all of us, of life's evolutional lesson.

REFLECTIONS

BREATHE

When feeling the stresses of life's constant chase,
Take a step back, and create yourself space,
Rushing and fretting, in the race of the rat,
Try to breathe purposely, being calm as you act,
The breath is the key, to living and for giving,
The in breath and out breath, inhale & uplifting,
The worries and frustrations, with no reason or rhyme,
A thief of your joy, and stolen moments in time,
The simplicity of breathing and respiratory,
Is a gift taken for granted, by you and by me,
So in moments of anger, or being put to the test,
Remember your safety net, and go back to the breath.

REFLECTIONS

FIX

Helping each other, is doing good deeds,
But be mindful of yourself, and your own needs,
It's great to help the world, saving who and all we can,
As long as we don't forget the fundamental, of "who I am",
We can get lost in the mix, of the broken ones who fall,
We can be on a pathway to fix, without looking at our flaws,
It's easy to distract ourselves, by transference of our issues,
The broken wing syndrome, a psychological mission,
It isn't easy to break habits, we unconsciously promote,
Helping others selflessly, but not to self-denote.
In the event of emergency, first put on your own mask,
These are aircraft instructions, the rules strictly ask,
How can you help another when you yourself are so unstable?
Look after number one & empower yourself able,
This way will help you, to look after more than one,
Your strength will inspire guidance, helping people move on.

REFLECTIONS

LENS

Looking through the lens of life, a unique view for all,
Differences and unity, choices between flight or fall,
Short-sighted with views, in a narrative way,
No tolerance for people, turning them away,
True beauty is missed, in this world as time passes,
True hatred is caught, with the rose-tinted glasses,
The lens that we hold, is the world as we know it,
Sometimes obscured, until we are shown it.
Life's pathway may unfold a colourful journey,
But it's the lens we perceive, whilst trying and learning,
We grow and we suffer, in our highs or the gutter,
We see joy from our pain, when our hearts start to flutter,
Our view is our distance of how we move forward,
Limited in our thoughts, then things become awkward,
So do a lens check, from time to time,
Not from an optician, but with the Divine,
A limitless energy of an eternal life force,
A power of all creation, the ultimate source,
Your lens is your life, your living story book,
Stood in the reality of truth, from where you look.
A beauty unquantified, can be seen and found,
From the lens of our soul, within and around.

REFLECTIONS

THE BEST OF YOU

Some people are encouragers and supporters in this life,
Whilst others are dictators and spectating with a knife,
We try our hardest to be the best in everything we do,
Some will be dismissive with… "is this the best you can do?"
Our best is never good enough, for those who refuse to see,
Our worst is what they wait for, and for us never to succeed.
When life is like the first line, going back to the start,
With souls who are truly wonderful, and have our best interests at heart,
They will say "it can be done!", and they help you be the best,
They will buckle up next to you, when life can be a test,
In life we must experience the good and the bad,
Not dwelling too much in the things that make us sad,
People are people and we learn to be discerning,
All the negatives and positives, it's all about learning,
So for those who say… it cannot be done,
Don't interrupt the person who's already begun.

REFLECTIONS

SCARS

At times we can look back, and see how life was hard,
Not only by the memories, but also by the scars,
The physical ones they say, are wounds of our wars,
Wars in life, our sabotage, the bricks thrown at our doors,
These are scars we look upon, to see how far we've come,
Once painful and traumatic, and still may be for some,
But it's the scars on our emotions, the ones you cannot see,
The hidden suffering of the mind, affecting you and me,
These scars cannot be covered up, or treated with a plaster,
They affect our lives in ways that can end up in disaster,
So whatever scars you hold, whether small, large or bold,
Physical or emotional, there's a story to be told.
Never be ashamed of the scars upon your body,
Or the ones in mind, share them with somebody,
Always be true, and let your light shine through,
As the war wounds of your past, is a testament to you.

REFLECTIONS

JOURNEY WITHIN

We have all come to this world, to be of service and of purpose,
It can take us different times, to accept our inner guidance,
Our vehicle is the soul, that takes us through this life,
The fuel is the spirit, with a power of guiding light.
Time becomes timeless, when we talk about the soul,
As this vehicle of experiences, makes our lives whole,
A magical carriage taking us, from this life to the next,
With a purpose unique to us, encouraging the best.
You can think you are just a body of bones, organs and skin,
But on searching much deeper, there's a soulful journey within.

REFLECTIONS

PEACE

Peace is a feeling, of a peace beyond all doubt,
Perfection and harmony, is not what it's all about,
The chaos and mess, that this life can bring,
Can destroy the peace within, that our hearts want to sing,
It's about being at ease, with the actions we take,
It's about being honest, in the mistakes that we make,
Sleeping with clear consciences, in all that we do,
Calming the storms, that life puts us through,
Peace is with nature, and sits with our soul,
The stillness within, is the ultimate goal,
The spring wouldn't curse summer, for coming too soon,
The sun wouldn't curse darkness, because it is lit by the moon,
The thunder, the lightening, the storms on the horizon,
The cause, the effects, of the deeds we decide on,
Life can be emotional, and we don't know where to begin,
But nature can teach us, true peace comes from within.

REFLECTIONS

Matador

For exclusive discounts on Matador titles,
sign up to our occasional newsletter at
troubador.co.uk/bookshop